Spots in a
Bad Mood

First published in 2008
by Wayland

Wayland
338 Euston Road
London NW1 3BH

Wayland Australia
Level 17/207 Kent Street
Sydney, NSW 2000

Series Editor: Louise John
Cover design: Paul Cherrill
Design: D.R.ink
Consultant: Shirley Bickler

A CIP catalogue record for this book is available from the British Library.

ISBN 9780750254038

Printed in China

Wayland is a division of Hachette Children's Books,
an Hachette Livre UK Company
www.hachettelivre.co.uk

Spots in a Bad Mood

Written by Karen Wallace
Illustrated by Lisa Williams

WAYLAND

B   7/08

Spots the Leopard woke up
in a bad mood.

The sun was too yellow.

The sky was too blue.

The jungle was too green.

Nothing was right.

Spots roared an angry roar and stomped around in a circle. Then he went and scratched all the bark off a tree.

"What's the matter with you?"
asked Lulu the Parrot.

Spots did not reply. He roared louder and ripped down the branch that Lulu was sitting on.

Poor Lulu! She squawked and flew away as fast as she could.

"When I'm in a bad mood, I swing back and forth," said Monty the Monkey. "It always makes me feel better."

14

15

"I'm not a monkey!" growled Spots.

He was very angry, and flicked his tail at Monty.

Monty fell over and banged his head on the ground.

"Stop being silly," said Flora the Elephant. "We are your friends. Why are you so nasty?"

But Spots didn't reply. "Go away,"
he shouted. "You're NOT my friends
any more."

"Let's play by ourselves," said Monty.
"I don't like Spots when he's in
a bad mood."

"Nor do we," said Flora and
Lulu together.

So they all went to play and left Spots alone in the jungle.

Spots sat all by himself
in the bushes.

He could hear his friends laughing,
but he couldn't see them.

They were playing hide and seek.
It was his favourite game!

Spots felt more and more lonely.

He knew had been mean and silly but now he wanted to have fun with his friends again!

So Spots went to find Monty and
Lulu and Flora.

"I'm sorry I've been silly," he said.
"I didn't mean to be nasty."

"That's okay, Spots," said Monty.
"Come and play hide and seek
with us!"

Suddenly Spots felt much better.
His bad mood had vanished!

"Follow me," he shouted. "I know
a really good place to hide!"

START READING is a series of highly enjoyable books for beginner readers. They have been carefully graded to match the Book Bands widely used in schools. This enables readers to be sure they choose books that match their own reading ability.

The Bands are:

Pink / Band 1
Red / Band 2
Yellow / Band 3
Blue / Band 4
Green / Band 5
Orange / Band 6
Turquoise / Band 7
Purple / Band 8
Gold / Band 9

START READING books can be read independently or shared with an adult. They promote the enjoyment of reading through satisfying stories supported by fun illustrations.

Karen Wallace was brought up in a log cabin in Canada. She has written lots of different books for children, fiction and non-fiction, and even won a few awards. Karen likes writing funny books because she can laugh at her own jokes! She has two sons and two cats. The sons have grown up and left home but the cats are still around.

Lisa Williams did her first drawing at 15 months old - it was a worm! She told her mum to write 'Worm' underneath the picture. When she was five, she decided that she wanted to be an illustrator when she grew up. She has always loved drawing animals and hopes that you will enjoy this book...